Again Behold the Stars

Alex Josephy

Cinnamon Press
:: small miracles from distinctive voices ::

Published by Cinnamon Press
Office 49019, PO Box 92, Cardiff, CF11 1NB.
www.cinnamonpress.com

The right of Alex Josephy to be identified as author of this work has been asserted by her in accordance with the Copyright, Designs and Patent Act, 1988. © 2021, Alex Josephy

ISBN 978-1-78864-138-8

British Library Cataloguing in Publication Data. A CIP record for this book can be obtained from the British Library.

All rights reserved. No part of this publication may be reproduced, stored in a retrieval system, or transmitted in any form or by any means, electronic, mechanical, photocopying, recording or otherwise without the prior written permission of the publishers. This book may not be lent, hired out, resold or otherwise disposed of by way of trade in any form of binding or cover other than that in which it is published, without the prior consent of the publishers.

Designed and typeset in Bodoni by Cinnamon Press. Cover design by Adam Craig Frontispiece artwork by Simon Turvey..

Cinnamon Press is represented by Inpress Ltd.

Acknowledgements

I wrote *Again Behold the Stars* in 2021, during and after the Covid 19 pandemic. Lockdown in the UK and in the small Italian hill town where I live got me thinking in a different way about medieval sieges in Italy, a history still very much alive in the minds of people who live there today. I was intrigued by stories of medieval women's frequent involvement and importance in defending their towns and enduring siege conditions.

Many European towns and city states were besieged during the 1500s. I haven't tried to chronicle our local siege in a connected way, but have drawn inspiration from its fragments. Some of these are mythical, or based on stories told by friends and neighbours. I also researched, stole and jigsawed in details from other places, in particular the siege of Siena, 1553-5, and I drew extensively on traditional local names, plants, geography and creatures. All the named characters and many of the events are fiction.

The structure of the sequence is based on the idea of 'scorci' - little glimpses of a landscape beyond, seen down a narrow channel between buildings. The poems are 'scorci'; they are linked glimpses, but the links between them are not made entirely explicit. I played with sonnet and madrigal forms to shape individual poems .

Special thanks are due to my inspiring, constructively critical and bilingual friends Lisa Maria Annicchiarico and Michelle Lovric, and to Claire Dyer for her invaluable mentoring.

I am also indebted to Alessandro Faneschi's *Montalcino, 1553. Cronaca di un assedio*, (Nuovi Voci, 2021), Isabella Dusi's *Vanilla Beans and Brodo* (Simon & Schuster, 2002) and Sandra Sider's *Handbook to Life in Renaissance Europe* (Oxford University Press, 2005).

The epigraphs in this book are drawn from David Hornbrook's English translation of *Giornale anonimo dell'Assedio di Montalcino fatto dagli Spagnuoli nel 1553*, the journal of an anonymous participant in the defence of Montalcino. The translation of an extract from Dante's Divine Comedy is my own.

Contents

Siege Girl	9
Blue	10
Wakeful	11
Nests	12
Water Soup	13
Redbreast	14
Kindling	15
Mulework	16
Redoubt	17
Chorus	18
Great Grandmother	19
A Prayer	20
Beyond	21
Purgatorio	22
Tartaruga	23
La Nebbia	24
Fawn	25
The One Tree	26
Mud, Dust, Ice, Stars	27
Rosso	28
Turn	29
Plough	30
Vulcano	31
Starlight	32
Straws	33

It's winter, 1553. A small Italian hill town is under siege, swept up in a power struggle between rival European forces. The townspeople are hugely outnumbered by their enemies, but the town has a fortress and high walls, and has never been taken in war.

Nothing great is ever achieved without much enduring.
St. Catherine of Siena

Again Behold the Stars

Siege Girl

Our enemies waited, dug themselves in,
unfolded their tents and pavilions.

A girl is always under siege,
always under guard, her own or others'.
Even when she thinks she's alone

her defences are probed, weaknesses
calculated, riches speculated, goods
greedily fantasised.

There's always someone's ladder pitched
in the lee of the watchtower, someone
itching to scale the curtain wall,

gain access to the keep. From the day
her fingers unfold, she clutches keys,
memorises passwords,

knows and estimates the next invaders
long before they decide to enlist.

Blue

On the two-hundredth day
she cuts a tangled blanket
from her long black hair.
Through an arrow window
the sky is tall, the valley wide;
her eyes stall
on distant woods, the blue
where her father fell.
Closer at hand, scarlet banners
flutter over ranked tents.
Spaniards. Florentines.
Ice has formed on every twig
of the holm oak. Grass stalks swell,
ferment in her belly.

Unlucky, an owl on the roof.
But this house belongs
to war. Has no roof.
Those inside are safe, unbreached
while they breathe. A girl can wait
in the shadow of the watch-wall,
ride the owl's hunting cries.
They wheel, girl and *gufo*,
into gimlet silence,
the blue hollow
before a kill. She sees
with *gufo* eyes, how the world
seethes. Everything is prey
and predator.

Wakeful

Squashed between three sisters
who wriggle like worms in a sack of grain,

she tries to sleep, covers her ears
against the brutal thud, thud:

boulders, hurled against the walls
from a wooden jaw, like those balls carved

from leftover chestnut stumps, flung
again and again by lads

with nothing to do on summer evenings.
Even the whine of marsh mosquitoes

would be welcome now.
She dreams of the tickling fingers

of her most annoying brother, sent out
in the dark to shore up frozen ditches.

Nests

I

Against the chapel lintel, earth vessels
no larger than thimbles
adhere. Their mouths are sealed
with a brown scale. She lays one ear
against the nearest, attentive
for the slightest rustle,
a wasp wing rearranged.

Nothing. Her eyes from lack of sleep
have become visionaries, pierce
the thin wall, share
for an instant the lair of
a torpid angel,
six legs cradled around
a promised miracle.

II

She keeps a secret: an abandoned nest
in the bramble thicket behind the sacristy
at San Francesco. She admires it
with a fingertip: softest chalice, laced
skeleton leaves, twigwork overlaid
with a cling of moss, ghost-green
and felted by a blackbird's breast.
From inside the building, tones rise and fall.
It's human song, the circling drone
of a long confession. A soldier sobs,
the priest answers every sin with a low
kindly rumble. Perhaps he's explaining
how there's a holy place, warm and rounded
ready for spring, just the other side of the wall.

Water Soup

Nor is there any green grass left,
we having eaten it all for salad.

Zia Carlina wields a ladle, taller
than her bent back. Worries
a broth over the fire, throws in
a brown sprinkle.
She calls it water soup.

The girl thickens this soup
with yellow wishes:
carrot ribbons, onion labyrinths,
sweet clouds of chestnut.

Carlina's fingers hover,
knots eased in the steam,
beckon the guards over
for merenda. Bowls of water
seasoned with last year's leaves.

Redbreast

In days when he was free
to roam outside the town,
Luca would paint *ornello* twigs
with pine-sap glue, to trap
musicians in the *bosco*:
blackbird, thrush, *Pettorosso*.

Held the moment they alighted,
wings ripped to ruin, they'd strain
one slender foot, then the other,
and keeping hope alive, cry out
for help in parched whistles,
rapid as their small hearts, till Luca

returned with knife and sack. Spiked,
roasted, oh, they made tender morsels.

Kindling

How would it be to eat a frozen twig?
A fingernail? A scorpion can live
all winter on nothing,
but does not grow.
Siege Girl's work this morning
is to walk in circles till she is warm
while her *nonna* empties
buckets of foul water over the wall,
her mother breaks
the milking stool into kindling.

Nevertheless, standing in the archway,
the girl stretches above her head
and for the first time, her fingers
brush the keystone.

Mulework

She carries two leather buckets
to and from the *pozzo*
at the *ospedale*; it's her trusted task
now her father's gone. The weight
drags her shoulders, drains
the pride from her neck. She groans,
sulky sister to the ox and the mule.
Nothing for it but to shuffle
up to the steeping cell, where wizened roots
and leaf bundles wait in the dark.
It's too far. Bitchy frost pinches
where her hand rags have unravelled.
What would Babbino say? '*Bambina
coraggiosa*, this is your cross.'

Redoubt

Three women's battalions, uniformed in red and violet
taffeta, fought on the city walls.

La Fortezza bares a stony
countenance. She gathers
the beseiged under her skirts.

Against her stubborn wall
the cannonballs shatter
like fishermen's glass floats,

leave no more than scratches.
Moss heals her. Sparrows roost
inside her scars. She glowers

from her high redoubt
beyond the mangled plain,
all the way to the sea

where boats cast off as easily
as taffeta slips from the loom.

Chorus

We cannot harm them except with boiled water and lime, which we pour down consistently... and we have let loose many swarms of bees on them, which give them no little discomfort.

'Listen, all you girls,' said blue-eyed Ugo,
sweat drooling from his beard
as the *nonni* hoisted stones against
a rampart, 'Did you hear
what they're calling you now?
Beccamorti—yes,
the death-detectors–those
who cluster round battle grounds,
eyes as clever as crows'—
those whose mystery is to peck
at corpse-flesh, bite the feet
of fallen bodies, shake life
into living men, to tell dead
from doggo.'

Ha! According to Silvana
the Florentines' faces are whipped arses!
Their heads are boiled-dry saucepans
crowned with cuckold horns.
'Yes, and their broken balls flap
in the breeze,' trills Ofelia
whose voice is like a throstle's.
'They call us *Beccamorti*? True!'
bellows Graziella. 'We're the Devil's
debt collectors, pecking over
what remains of those *mortacci*.'
'Even whores,' whispers Valentina,
who has been to the Maremma,
'scorn their teeny *piselli*, their stinking florins.'

Great Grandmother

A young girl lives inside Bisnonna.
She's besieged by a body
that has weathered eighty winters,
Tramontana wind, hail and sun,
has no use for *misericordia*.
Under skin, a second line
of attack: a cramp of iron muscles
forged by walking the hill. Aches
bombard her, cares dig trenches,
starve and ravine her cheeks.
Even the laughing days cast nets
around her neck.
   The wise girl waits,
watchful, behind fading blue shutters
she keeps almost closed.

A Prayer

Lady, help us heave the bodies
of our sacrificed soldiers, pierced
by wicked arrows, over the wall
into the cold embrace
of mountain air.

Let them spill dread
on sleeping mercenaries.
Send our orphaned tears
streaming down the gutters
that gush from the oxen trough
above the ravine.

Pour all our sorrow
to the last poisonous drip
onto the enemy.

Beyond

At dawn, the distant mountain
is a blue woman, resting
belly up on pillows of snow.
Her breath makes frosty plumes;
she hums across the sky.

Our valley sags under the invaders.
Ditches are sumps where flesh
and soil congeal; broken tree limbs
bristle like weaponry. Fields howl,
become mouths of mines; red clay
stands up out of a boar's wallow, gathers
into squads that lurch at our walls.

At dusk, the mountain is a blue woman
adorned with silver where her drifts lie deep.

Purgatorio

Weep if you want to. Tears
are just salty water,

and mud and water
make a handy bowl.

Flour and water
swell miraculous loaves

and wine and water
remind us to sing.

This frost is water, held
for a spell in icy prison.

Inside the hill, naiads
keep their kettles.

The town has wells deeper
and older than our tears.

Tartaruga

I

Nonna's tortoise walked in the sun
before the siege began. I saw him slit
two eyelids, squint for yellow petals,
and how in delight at finding them, a third lid
flickered to and fro, a cloudy leaf
of veined alabaster cut wafer thin
like those windows in Sant'Antimo
where you catch a glimpse of paradise,
but it's really just a dusty olive grove.

How does a *tartaruga* breathe?
The stone armour that shelters me
constricts my soul. These walls
bruise the hand that beats them, flatly refuse
to be anything except limestone blocks.

II

Giulia tells her of a war tortoise
that might even now be shambling
across the plain: under a carapace
of welded shields, a brainless butting head
to shiver gates, tear down the walls.
They plan their own *tartaruga*: an oak frame
taken from the ruined hens' shelter, armoured
with Nonna's roasting bowls, pimpled
with cauldrons and the scalded moonface
of the chestnut pan. Inside their ugly ark
they'll cram a nightmare worse than any
clanking siege machine: a pitiless squadron
of mothers, little sisters, wives
with nothing but sad stories left to lose.

La Nebbia

Cold mist has swallowed everything
beyond the siege: farms with their chapels,
crossroads, bridges, brown seed bunches
on *ornello* trees. Before, there was the market
in the valley, donkeys on the pilgrim way,
porcupines humping toward shelter.
All are cancelled; mist inflates in her head.
She grasps at fragments, broken tiles
to add together: green archipelago,
cloud pines lapped by waves, white
like dead soldiers' hands; the *Roccaforte*
on the next hill, yellow rocks that glow
above the cloud. She sees it's a blessing,
a stone ship becalmed, set free from battle.

Fawn

She coils it round her neck
against a bitter wind: the shawl
her friend from the mountain gave her
at the mushroom harvest.

Dusted with pink threads at the edge
of green, the shawl is like a field
in early March, a shy reveal of sap,

the raised pelt of a fawn,
warm air sliding its hands
across the flat land from the sea.

How long can it be since they met?
The colours are less clear
with every wash: field, fawn
and friend, fading to grey.

The One Tree

How she misses the company of chestnut woods
leaves arched   above her head
like cockerels' fancy tail-feathers
prickling shells   to hurl at teasing brothers

Chestnut rafters steady the house
buckets take on curves   in Nonno's workshop
chestnut broth   soothes her throat in dreams
chestnut bread   haunts her tongue

She visits the one tree in the barren orto
fungus swells in the underbark   where beetles gnaw
intricate galleries   inside, the tree endures

Fallen leaves rug the winter woods
crushed underfoot   smell sweetly brown
carry chestnut *amicizia*   through February.

Mud, Dust, Ice, Stars

Muddy puddles near the *fonte*,
where her sisters jump and stamp,
craze into brown ice stars.
Smooth mud pulled from a bank,
pummelled and pinched, grows legs
and horns. They leave their clay cuckolds
tucked between loaves in the *forno*
when Ofelia's not looking. Later
they paint the dolls with red mud slime,
give them *cacca moustaches*, call them
Captain, Enemy. Mud is anything
you want it to be: a spy's tally of passers-by;
an ally when it clogs hooves, stops time,
raises the price of a small hill town.

Between baking and confession
she finds a sheltered hideyhole
at the mouth of a *vicolo*,
picks up a rook's feather,
makes sketches in the dust:
round Sun rayed like a smiling lion;
sky orb; a world that leaps
like a hare in loopy circles; stars
spinning free from their spheres
—or is that sin? She's carrying too many
already, what with the slapped baby,
the stolen sip of best grappa. Scratches it out,
draws a small girl in a square piazza, wide
and flat as the good Lord's palm.

Rosso

Carried to the ramparts,
dark red wine unlocks everything:
hearts, frosted fingers, history.

They hand her a beaker, water
tinged pink as if a warm September
has dissolved there

or a small thrush
has shared the last of its life.

Before parlay with the Spanish
the captain smears his ashen cheeks
with wine, like a woman's
unholy *belletto*. To show how well we do.

'Excellent use of wine!' admit the archers,
and even the priest.

Turn

We climbed, he first, I following,
until I glimpsed through a round opening
all the lovely things the sky holds.
So we emerged, again beheld the stars.
                    Dante: Inferno, Canto XXXIV

Luca, Piero and Elvio like to sing
like captive *uccellini*, madrigals
a cappella, for comfort after dark.

Three voices twine and separate:
bear buzz partners flute call; each verse
twizzles the tune, turns the story.

In one, the Virgin throws a blue cloak round the town,
shines her gaze on the enemy; astounded,
the Viceroy's horse falls to its knees, vanquished.

In others less sublime, a treaty
bamboozles both armies, or the chests
of dukes are emptied of soldi

and everyone goes home, and for a time
there will be songs, and boasts, and bandages.

Plough

Her *nonno* made this wooden angel
fallen to earth just beyond her reach
outside the walls. She can see it
from the secret gate by the *corniolo* tree.
It rests one tooled and handled wing
gently against a rock. The other
flares into the sky. Its head
like any angel's, is serene.
It narrows to a tip, tilted to slide

through the most stubborn mysteries,
most stoney tilth; Nonno's craft coaxed fields
out of scrub. She stops to check
it's still there, the plough he carved
and forged, the month she was born.

Vulcano

Oneglia says a dragon
sleeps inside the mountain.
She remembers women at the spring
that boils from the cave;

their hair was all one floating cloth,
their limbs were dragon steam,
hot purple like *calaminta*.
She recalls a boy who tumbled

when the dragon rattled the white rocks
by the waterfall. How his little leg
was splintered, how it took two men
to carry him, *pian piano*

to float in the dragon's pool.
How every splinter healed.

Starlight

A siege can drag on past childhood
into a life. At each turn of the year,
siege-songs spool new verses;
Purgatorio is a book of hours, stretched
to maddening length, soon forgotten.
There's pride in water soup, rage
in the release of bees from a battlement,
consolation in smuggled grain and gossip.

In the house of war she thrives
under many-coloured stars. Some nights
they sail so close, she can see how everything
will be worn down, ploughed under, pitted
like the poor moon's face, but brighter
than before, when this is over.

Straws

There's no good news from the watchmen

but her aunt Carlina has chosen names
for when the baby comes: Agnella, little lamb,
fresh ewe's cheese in a straw basket. If it's *un maschio*,
then Giulio, knowing nothing but joy.

The girl counts vacant swift nests anchored
to the tower, crescent husks
that wait like fishing skiffs
on vertical stone sea.

Her mother made the shoes
she binds with corn stalks where they purse
darkened lips to taste the weather.
She walks in their kiss.

No news, but dry grass gleams all down the hill.

www.ingramcontent.com/pod-product-compliance
Ingram Content Group UK Ltd.
Pitfield, Milton Keynes, MK11 3LW, UK
UKHW041342280325
456815UK00002B/92